In the land of temples

By the same author:

A new biology of religion: spiritual practice and the life of the body

The fiction of a thinkable world: body, meaning, and the culture of capitalism

Our wilderness: how the people of New York found, changed, and preserved the Adirondacks

In the land of temples:

Notes from a South Indian pilgrimage

Michael Steinberg

Rochester, New York 2012

*All text and images copyright © 2011-2012 Michael Steinberg,
except for the image of the deities at the Chennai Maha Pratyangira Temple,
which was scanned from an image purchased from a nearby vendor.*

ISBN: 978-1-105-70370-6

Table of Contents

A temple not built by human hands..1

Goddesses of charm and power..23

Traffic school...47

The dance of Shiva...69

If you were asked where ancient spiritual traditions are still alive in everyday life you might well answer Tibet. But South India has an equal claim to this distinction; it has been called the land of temples and the last surviving classical civilization. On holy days processions clog the streets as the gods and goddesses are pulled through their domain on intricately carved chariots, and its thousands of sacred sites still draw throngs on festival days and business days alike. The crowds are largest in December, when the highways and side roads are filled with busloads of pilgrims taking advantage of the good weather. In 2011 I was one of them. This is some of what I saw.

A temple not built by human hands

Thiruvannamalai, Tamil Nadu

In the land of temples, page 5

India may be a place where travelers see what they choose to see, but it tends to frustrate romantic ideals as often as it satisfies them. Dreams of the Indian temple town, for example, evaporate on first contact; you might as well expect to encounter the divine in a bus station. But that's only because most of us have a limited, even prissy idea of what the divine is like and how it gets encountered. Our common idea of holiness is still stuck on the old saw about cleanliness being next to godliness. It shares far too much with the manicured tidiness of Shangri La in the movie *Lost Horizon*. We expect a lot of greenery, blue skies, a few well-placed vistas of grandeur or at least charm, and a pervasive air of peace, joy, and oneness with creation. People should speak in hushed voices and draw close to the sanctuary with quiet steps. (You don't run or walk to these sanctuaries, you're supposed to draw near them, bonelessly almost, as if you're being sucked in by the gentlest of tractor beams.) There's no architecture or greenery at all in the closing scene of Terrence Malick's *The Tree of Life* but it's the same old vision, chock-a-block with the soft sounds of nature, calm you can cut with a knife, hushed voices, and beautiful souls being swept bonelessly to the light.

Wherever *The Tree of Life* ends up, it's definitely not India. Holiness there is both more common and less dressed up. Take, for example, the town of Thiruvannamalai. Few places in the south are more sacred. It sits at the base of Arunachala hill, a half-mile-high extinct volcano that is said to be not merely the abode of Lord Shiva but a manifestation of the great god himself. Pilgrims come to Thiruvannamalai to walk the Girivalam, the fourteen kilometer path that circles the sacred mountain, to see the god in his great temple in the center of town, and to visit the ashram of the sage Ramana Maharshi, whose death in 1950 was marked by a ball of light that rose from Arunachala and passed over much of Tamil Nadu before it reached the sea. I myself have come here with a hundred other devotees, planning to do all of these. And the first things I notice are the dust, the diesel fumes, the special intensity of the traffic noise, and the hip-hop style street ads for a brand of *lungi*, the sarong-like wrap that is the traditional men's garb in this part of the world.

There are quiet side streets in Thiruvannamalai. The ashrams are indeed hushed and Sri Ramana's is even picturesque. Almost nothing else in the town, though, suggests the kind of holiness that Hollywood portrays and Protestant megachurches aspire to—aside from the billboard for a gated community which promises purchasers a chance to "live at feet of Lord." It's a crowded, dusty, messy place, like many Indian towns, and hardly anything about it is conventionally pretty or even attractive. It has none of the woods, water, and open space that enliven Chennai and little traditional and no colonial architecture. It's a chaos of blocky concrete buildings devoted to retail of all sorts set in a maze of streets totally unsuited to the masses of cars, autorickshaws, and tour buses which dodge or ignore traffic signs and traffic barricades alike. It is also alive with the peculiarly public energy of Indian life, which can lift your spirits far above the garbage on the crumbling sidewalks and the constant noise of car horns. None of it, though—good, bad, or beyond good and evil—seems particularly conducive to an encounter with the divine.

But then there is the temple. The "big temple," it's sometimes called, to distinguish it from the dozens of small temples scattered throughout the town; but you could just as easily call it *the* temple. It's unavoidable. Its 24 acres stretch for blocks in the center of Thiruvannamalai, a huge rectangle whose giant gray stone walls remind me incongruously of a prison. Instead of barbed wire on top, though, there is statue after identical statue of a reclining bull. This is Nandi, Shiva's mount and his most devoted worshiper, whose love for his master is so great that he himself is now counted as a god. And instead of watchtowers there are *gopurams*, the main ones more than twenty stories high.

The *gopuram* is the most distinctive feature of the South Indian temple, so much so that it's become a kind of symbol for the region. In the north the tallest part of a temple is likely to be the sanctuary. This makes sense, because the temple is the home of a god (or gods) and the gods live in high places, by preference the Himalaya. Temples up north are artificial mountains. In the south, though, the guiding metaphor seems to be the palace, and the fortified gates found in human palaces evolved there to become wedge-shaped sculpture-encrusted towers. The sanctuary itself is most often a pillared hall only one or two stories high.

In the land of temples, page 8

You can glimpse the big temple's *gopurams* from far off, but to get to the one marking the main entrance we have to walk around two sides of the complex; our three buses can't find parking spots any closer. It's night already, the soft evening of the tropics, but our way is bright from the street lighting, the strings of bare bulbs that hang from the stalls along the temple wall, and light from the open shops across the way. Devotees and pilgrims surge in both directions as motorcyclists and autorickshaw drivers pick their ways artfully through the crowds. People stop to consider what's for sale: sacred pictures, fried snacks, garlands of fresh flowers and other offerings to be brought to the gods, toys for restless children or those left behind while mother and father are away, colored powders, bangles, cords, and necklaces of the crinkled red-brown *rudraksha* beads sacred to the god, said to be the tears that Shiva wept as he flew around the world with the dead body of his first wife in his arms. From a CD shop I hear the honey-sweet voice of playback singer S.P. Balasubramaniam singing "Om namah Shivaya." (On a later visit a friend and I dash in to buy the CD, four long tracks for 50 rupees, about a dollar.)

Once we reach the entrance, though, we step out of the riot of noise, color, and garish artificial light into something else. We file past a security guard who seems to ignore the video game sounds of his magnetometer and then massages our bags in a strictly pro forma manner. He does not find my camera—photography is forbidden inside the sanctuaries and often frowned-upon elsewhere—but it makes no difference. Inside is a waking dream, the hidden divine nature of reality manifest in stone. I am not in a mood to take pictures.

The first courtyard is vast and the next one seems even bigger. From the *gopurams* and the roofs of all the secondary temples gods, spirits, and ordinary humans look down on us or go about their business without noticing our fleeting lives. A giant black Nandi gazes lovingly in the direction of the sanctum, still far away. We are hardly the only visitors but all around is space, so much space that the noise of the other devotees is all but lost.

Everything in me falls silent. I understand now what it means to be awestruck, though the words that come of their own bidding are less poetic. Holy shit, I think. My thoughts, my feelings, spin in a tight circle. I want to do nothing but drink in the air, the stillness, the sense of presence that is palpable and close to overwhelming even this far from the heart of the compound.

In the half light the black granite buildings merge into the shadows like looming thoughts in the landscape of a dream. As in some dreams, each courtyard leads through to another and another, more walls and more *gopurams*, taking us ever deeper as we draw near the home of the god. At each gateway we step up and down and touch the worn stone threshold to take its dust on our heads and hearts, submitting ourselves to the temple's own logic and power as we move towards the sanctuary.

I feel as if I am walking through something built long before there were people. The time-smoothed cut stone walls, the tiers of corniced niches and statues, the smaller temples inside the complex with their own teeming superstructures, all seem to have grown here through oceanic time, far too complex and inevitable to be the work of human hands.

We honor elephant-headed Ganesh, as you must at the start of any Hindu ritual, but the pilgrimage organizers are in a hurry and I don't get much of a look at the sanctuary itself before we are inside of it. There is plenty to distract me inside, though, because I am once again face to face with the Indian refusal to turn the sacred into something pretty and presentable. The huge two-storied hallways, dark or age-darkened stone held up by ornately-carved pillars, are lit by bare fluorescent bulbs. As we enter we are channeled into a system of metal rails right out of Disneyland. On the walls and hanging from the ceilings are large blue signs with white letters in Tamil and English directing people to Ordinary Darshan and Special Darshan. People are lining up obediently. There's something factory-like about the scene.

Darshan—ordinary or special—is what we're here for. The word means "sight," and taking darshan means literally that we get to see the divinity. But sight means something different in India than it does in the West. I was taught that perception is something passive; we open our eyes and receive and process whatever image falls on our retinas. And what we process is merely an image, a shadow of the real world that remains outside of us and quite apart from us. We look out from our selves into a world which we know only by image and inference.

Traditionally, at least, Indians have interpreted vision differently. It's something active. We project ourselves out into the world, they say, and what we see is what comes back to us. Perception, then, is interaction. When two people exchange glances each one picks up a bit of the other's being; they stand in each other's shoes. While this theory isn't consistent with the physics of vision, it shows a much better grasp of the actual neurological processes; in reality, imagination, intention, perception, and understanding are all intermingled. In an important sense the Indians are right and we're wrong; perception is not passive at all.

That's why exchanging glances with the gods is so important. We become divinized, just a little, and the gods become just a touch humanized. One could argue that none of this is necessary. According to the tradition that my home temple follows, there is no essential difference between gods and people. So what is the use of temples or of darshan?

They're still necessary, at least for most of us, because we find it all but impossible to experience that lack of separation. Reality is one, but we live in pieces. In the temple, at least, and in the moment of darshan, those of us who aren't sages have a chance to breathe in that oneness. They're places where it's possible for ordinary people to live in the real world, if only for a few seconds.

Arrangements have been made for our group to have special darshan, so we move off to the right as the other devotees take the line to the left. In the end we will sit just outside the sanctum while they stand behind us. It is a mark of the hierarchical nature of Indian society, so deeply ingrained that nobody seems to mind. As our line and the ordinary darshan line pass next to each other we file along beside groups of peasant women wearing deep red cotton saris, devotees of the nearby goddess at Melmalayanur. Smiles pass back and forth but we're all too engrossed in chanting and in preparing ourselves for what comes next for anything more. We turn to the left, climb a few stairs, and find ourselves in a tiny room. It is stiflingly hot. The doors close behind us, and a brief ritual begins.

The focus of our attention is a lingam—the pillar-like object that is at the heart of almost every Shiva temple. Often called a phallic symbol, it is both more and less than that; in India sexual desire is just a specific instance of the universal dance of separation, yearning, and reunification. There are millions of lingams in thousands of temples, but the one in Thiruvannamalai is special. It is a *butalinga*, a lingam in which the divine manifests itself as one of the five elements of Indian cosmology: earth, water, fire, air, and space. This one is fire, though Arunachala itself is also a lingam of fire, and once a year it is lit up with a giant blaze that lasts for days and is seen for miles.

And what happens next? From one perspective it is nothing much. As we look through a doorway a priest waves a flame at the lingam, which is crowned with gold, shaded by a sculptured canopy of auspicious serpents, and draped in flower garlands. The priest mumbles a few words in Sanskrit and then comes out, giving us a chance to wave our hands over the same fire and handing us a pinch of *vibhuti*, the sacred ash.

Yet it feels nothing like that. The presence is the room is more intense than anything else I have ever experienced. There is a kind of electrical charge that connects us with the silent and self-contained energy of the lingam itself; like some elemental forces it seems all the stronger for the distance between the two. As I wave my hands over the flame, dab ash on my forehead and swallow what remains I can feel that energy passing into me. I have had darshan.

Then it is over, and the doors open again so the next group can come in. I walk down the steps into yet another grand pillared hall and I start laughing. It is somehow as if I had glimpsed the very creation of the world and that I was carrying it with me on my forehead and my tongue. I have no idea how that is possible. But isn't that the point?

Thenupureeshwara Temple, Tamil Nadu

Thenupureeshwara Temple, Tamil Nadu

Thenupureeshwara Temple, Tamil Nadu

Thenupureeshwara Temple, Tamil Nadu

Goddesses of charm and power

Nemili, Tamil Nadu

In the land of temples, page 27

Ours is basically a Shiva temple, our guru Aiya has said, although our worship is directed towards the goddess. This isn't as inconsistent as it might sound. In our tradition, at least, divinity has no gender. Absolute reality is beyond all separation and distinction, beyond subject and object even, so of course it's beyond male and female. But there's a catch (there's always a catch), which is that we can't ever know absolute reality as it is. To know something is to make it into an object, and it also means making ourselves into subjects, which is the other side of the coin so it's just as bad. What it would be like to be beyond subject and object is simply unavailable to us; as humans we're stuck in a world of separations and distinctions. So the original oneness-we-can't-even-call-oneness is always at least two by the time we get to it. Reality for us is always already splintered. That's why there's no inconsistency in running a Shiva temple where the goddess gets the devotion. Whichever one we worship, we're actually orienting ourselves towards something else, something that isn't and can't ever be a thing at all and that's both god and goddess and neither god nor goddess.

Still, most people figure they ought to choose between the two, because in the Indian world god and goddess set us on different paths—even though they end up in the same (no)place. Gods are male and the male is passive, contemplative, the embodiment of pure consciousness. You might think of Shiva, the ascetics' role model, sitting in endless meditation on Mount Kailash.

If you're the sort who divides spirit from matter the male is spirit. (Our tradition doesn't do this, but others do.) The female, on the other hand, is active, creative, restless and energetic. The (male) gods can do nothing alone; each one acts only through his consort, his *shakti*. In an untranslatable Sanskrit pun, Shiva without Shakti is *shava*—a corpse. For dualists the female is matter. In our tradition the female is absolutely everything. As she says in one text, she is the illusion of the world *and* the cure for that illusion.

This makes the goddess a very slippery character and the goddess path a treacherous one. Goddess worship is a deep strain in Indian culture, probably long predating the Vedas themselves, which means that it's untold thousands of years old. But like women and female sexuality in general, the goddess in Hindu tradition has always been viewed as both alluring and dangerous.

In India these contradictory aspects get projected into two kinds of goddesses. The first kind is (usually) married. Like our temple's deity, who is "the beautiful one in the three worlds," she's demure, beautiful, gracious, and loving. The other kind of goddess is single. Often a warrior who exults in battle, she's demanding, violent, and sometimes even vicious. She likes blood. Her vision cuts right to the heart. She commands absolute surrender.

The warlike goddesses are powerful allies, and their terms are nothing too onerous if you're really interested in the reality of things. But they make people uncomfortable, especially men, and a lot of effort has been put into taming them. In the temple city of Kanchipuram, a typically noisy and dusty Tamil Nadu town that was once the capital of the great Chola empire, sits the temple of Kamakshi Amman, one of the benevolent forms of the goddess. ("Amman" means "mother.") Not far away is another, much smaller temple, popularly called "Adi Kamakshi," the home of the original or first Kamakshi. The first Kamakshi has fangs. They're hard to see; Adi Kamakshi herself is now in a subsidiary shrine and she's safely behind bars most of the time. But everyone knows that they're there.

It's not that the benevolent goddesses are wimps. A few days after our trip to Thiruvannamalai we drove through fields and rice paddies edged with

In the land of temples, page 29

coconut palms to the small and rather pleasant town of Nemili. Nemili's chief distinction is that it's the home of Bala Tripurasundari, the goddess as a nine-year-old. ("Bala" means "little" in Tamil.) She doesn't have a temple there, though. Bala came to Nemili as a kind of house guest, and she's stayed on for a century and a half. She lives in an ordinary house on an ordinary side street, next door to a primary school, distinguished from the other houses on the street only by a small painted sign identifying itself as the Nemili Bala Peetam —Bala's residence in Nemili.

The story is lovingly recounted to all visitors. A hundred and fifty years ago Subramanya Iyer, the father of the family, had a dream visitation from Rajarajeshwari, the same goddess we worship in Rochester. I am coming to be with you, she said; go down to the river and I'll be there. Greatly excited, he and his family and their friends go to the river bank, where of course nothing happens. In stories like this nothing *ever* happens on the first day.

Each day more skeptics and disbelievers drift away and each night the goddess reassures Subramanya that she is only testing him. And on the third day, just as he is about to return home alone, a tiny gold figure washes up into his hands. It is Bala. She has come to his house, he learns, to rest. She is not averse to visitors, but nobody comes to see her unless she wants them to come. It turns out that she is not so unlike other nine-year-olds; her favorite offerings are candies and cookies.

Over time Bala has become more than the family's guest. The goddess has become almost a member of the family, speaking through one of the women, and she seems to have become the family business, too. The Nemili Bala Peetam is a busy place, and there's a considerable crowd watching as our group, a hundred strong, files in for our visit. We walk down a long, dark hallway and enter the peetam proper, a large t-shaped space put together from what must once have been several rooms. We pass a sales counter to our right. On the opposite wall, under the stairs, is a small Christmas tree. Light streams in from a courtyard on the far right and to our left, filling an entire wall, is a large and elaborate altar.

Our temple in Rochester has had a long-standing relationship with the Nemili Bala Peetam and we are welcomed as honored guests. The entire family comes out to meet us and the younger daughters sing for us, shuffling with shyness. There is quite an elaborate program; we are promised songs, a puja, and a sumptuous lunch. First, however, we are served coffee and biscuits.

The puja itself is a touching affair. Although one of the elders is a poet (we are handed a newspaper clipping and a plaque honoring him as the premier poet in Tamil) nobody seems to have the Sanskrit expertise to perform a puja in traditional form. Instead, the ritual offerings—flowers, incense, flames, food, and the camphor *arati* light—are accompanied by a mix tape which intersperses Sanskrit chants with the deliciously catchy devotional pop music that is one of the most endearing elements of South Indian culture. The whole scene feels domestic rather than awe-inspiring, and that is exactly the point. The homelike atmosphere is exactly what has drawn Bala here.

After lunch, which is indeed sumptuous, I have a chance to come close to the altar. According to the story Bala is no bigger than your middle finger, but she is even smaller than that. She is the size of my little finger, a strange gold figurine that seems vaguely African. Something about her reminds me of the famous dancing girl from the Harappan civilization, the mysterious first great culture of the distant Indian past, which many scholars think is where the cult of the goddess began.

Bala Tripurasundari stands in a diorama-like shelter with an idealized rural backdrop. The scene must be meant to evoke the landscape where the goddess came to Subramanya Iyer and transformed his life and those of his descendents.

In the land of temples, page 32

It looks a little like a black-velvet painting, I think, but what I'm noticing more than anything else is an unaccountable yet unmistakable sense of presence. I've been feeling it on and off throughout our visit. The tiny figure of Bala draws one in, and the half-improvised devotions and almost suburban plainness of the Peetam intensify her power instead of dispersing it. Beneath Bala's charm there is steel.

A few days later we visit another home of the goddess, this one, too, a little out of the mainstream. It is a temple to Maha Pratyangira, a particularly ferocious manifestation of the goddess in which she has the head of a lion. (Her name is pronounced "pra-TING-ger-uh.") In the first days of our pilgrimage Aiya had conducted a Pratyangira *homam,* a fire offering, a spellbinding ritual in which the goddess is offered red chilies and the mantra is itself peppered with the explosive syllable *phat.* Devotion to Maha Pratyangira is rare, however, and there are only a handful of temples anywhere in the world where she is the main deity.

The temple we have come to see is in a suburb to the south of Chennai, and to reach it we pass through the center of Chennai's high-tech world: the leafy campus of the Indian Institute of Technology-Madras, with its walls and security checkpoints, the big new office blocks for firms like PayPal and ebay, and shops for the new Indian middle class with names like "Mom & Me" alongside long-established restaurants, most of them vegetarian, which for reasons I cannot fathom are called "hotels" here.

We turn left off the main road, pass through a toll barrier, and stop. A dirt road stretches off to our right. The air is fresh and the humidity is high; we can't be too far from the Bay of Bengal, I think. The evening light and the hint of salt water give the site a pleasurable expansiveness, though they also draw mosquitoes; I worry that I neglected to put on insect repellant..

At the end of the road is the temple, its *gopuram* under construction or renovation;, covered by scaffolding with thatched walls. Off to one side is a line of semi-improvised sheds with the usual range of temple merchandise. Since this is not quite the ordinary temple, the usual range is a bit extended here;

there are garlands of turmeric for sale along with the flowers. On the other side is a brand-new building announced as "suitable for all functions," the Sri Varahi Mini Hall.

It is New Years' Day, an auspicious time to visit temples. Families are taking tiffin on the road side and the line for darshan stretches almost to the highway. It must take an hour or more to get inside unless you've made arrangements beforehand, as our group did. And there, right in front of us, visible and striking even a block away, is Sri Varahi herself. She is one of the Matrikas, a group of seven or eight mother-goddesses who evoke war and uncontrollable emotion. I have read that she has the head of a sow or a boar, but I have no problem deciding which one it is. Boars are far more dangerous than sows, and though the Varahi here sits demurely in her sari and is garlanded with flowers, there is no mistaking the ferocity in her silent black granite massiveness. She seems the essence of danger. Our temple's tradition sees her as the commander-in-chief of the divine armies, but I can't help feeling that she is a worrisome being to have around regardless of whose side she is on. I can't keep my eyes off her.

Around the corner from Varahi we get a better view of the temple. It is not an old temple and the founding priest is from Kerala, not Tamil Nadu. Thanks to his influence the individual shrines are in Keralan style, with pagoda-like red tile roofs. By most of the shrines are large signs in Tamil which identify the deity and give the appropriate mantras. This is something unusual, too. Mantras are generally kept secret, their power entrusted to the deserving few. Here, on the other hand, anyone who reads Tamil is invited to chant.

Most of the temple is covered by a corrugated steel roof of the sort used to shelter construction material in the U.S., but the grounds still give the impression of a garden with the gods set in their separate pavilions. What a garden it is, though! One great strength of Hinduism is its acknowledgment that the price of creation is pain and hurt, that life and death are two sides of the same coin, and that we can never be released from suffering until we embrace it. Even the most terrifying goddess can be addressed as "Ma," because the violence she embodies is like medicine, distasteful but necessary. The Maha Pratyangira temple is filled with goddesses, and just about all of them are there to remind us of those unpalatable truths. Maternal or not, their presence makes for the most disturbing garden I've ever walked into.

At one end there is a polychrome statue of Bhadrakali, a form of Kali widely worshiped in Kerala. She is said to be an auspicious and beneficent form but here she's thirty feet tall and green-skinned, her tongue lolls down as Kali's usually does—when she first appears Kali starts lapping up the blood of a demon—and like Adi Kamakshi she has fangs. The severed heads that form her necklace are huge. She, too, is a frightening and magnetic presence. Behind her, on the back wall of the shrine, are steps for the priests who every now and then pour offerings on her. I am surprised that they can keep on their feet.

Next to Bhadrakali stands a fire pit and a giant full-color statue of Agni, the god of fire. Lord Shiva comes next. He is another of the temple's main deities, so like Varahi he's in black granite, but here he is almost unrecognizable. He's shown in the half-bird, half-lion form of Sharabha, more powerful than any lion and the tamer of Vishnu's half-lion avatar Narasimbha. Rearing up on his hind legs he stares balefully at devotees with huge eyes set in a saucerlike face. His wings look more like those of an insect than of a bird.

Last, of course, comes Maha Pratyangira herself. She is at the western end of the temple, the most auspicious location, directly opposite Bhadrakali. Like Sharabha she, too, faces us and fixes us with her eyes. A crest of serpents covers her fanged leonine head as she roars silently out over her worshipers. Her four arms are filled with weapons; unlike many deities she makes no gesture that allays our fears. She is fear itself.

I hesitate to come much closer, but I step forward as the priest presents the light to her and to me and offers me a pinch of the blood-red *kumkum*. I put some on my forehead and wrap the rest in a scrap of newspaper. But it's also hard to move away. She, Sharabha, and Varahi haunt me as I walk back towards the bus. They haunt me still.

But what is it that haunts me? What had I seen? At first I thought that I had seen myself as the plaything of sheer, implacable, uncompromising power.. I am no longer so sure. As I walk back through the temple in my mind's eye the same shock returns, the same fear in the pit of my stomach, but it seems now that the ferocity that I sense and draw back from is my own. It is the angry, threatened intensity with which I guard every illusion that I cling to, from the ego on down, everything which keeps me from living in the real world. The gaze of Varahi, Sharabha's blunt scrutiny, and the deafening silent roar of Maha Pratyangira herself are my own attachments, purified and turned back at their source. They become a challenge, a demand that I do what I know must be done. They tell me the same message that the poet Rilke heard from another deity, the torso of Apollo—a god who resembles Shiva in mysterious ways. There is no place that does not see you, he said. You must change your life.

Adi Kamakshi Temple, Kanchipuram, Tamil Nadu

Adi Kamakshi Temple, Kanchipuram, Tamil Nadu

Shankaracharya of Kanchipuram, Tamil Nadu

Kanchipuram, Tamil Nadu

Traffic school

Evening traffic, Chennai

In the land of temples, page 51

There are people who go to India hoping for some kind of spectacular miracle. I was not one of them. I'm sure it would have been wonderful to see a spirit being materialize or dematerialize by my side as I walked around Arunachala or to have my ego melt away like ice, but you can't go into a situation with expectations like those, not even an Indian situation. I don't believe in miracles anyway, and I'm not even sure what I think about the paranormal. I believe what I see.

I try not to think about what I might see before I see it, though, and I guess I did hope for the unexpected when I set out. I was not disappointed in this. *Something* happened to me in those temples. It seems to be very much the same something that happens to many other people, and I'm happy to accept it as a real experience of something real. I'd just rather not talk about what that something might be. I'd rather let it work its way into the texture of my everyday life and find out how the world feels and works in its light.

And I did hope for something else beyond the spiritual, if that's what you want to call it. I wanted to walk out of the door of my hotel into a world with distinct ways of doing things. I wanted to discover aspects of life that were hidden or forgotten in the West. That was one reason that I had made the trip. It was also one of the reasons that had led me to our temple in Rochester and why I now call myself a Hindu if someone asks. I was not whoring after strange gods, as the Hebrew bible so nastily puts it. I did not come to believe that Sri Rajarajeswari or Lord Shiva was the real deity and Yahweh an imposter or a

In the land of temples, page 52

delusion. Instead, it felt to me that the traditions that venerated these figures embodied a particular world, and the world I had glimpsed through them felt much more like reality than the world that I had been born into.

Not that I wanted India to be exotic. The exotic is something you enjoy because it's strange and different and hard to understand. It's life at arm's length, a way of turning experience into entertainment. Nor did I want to pick up a taste for a few bits of local color—though I did return with a craving for South Indian breakfast foods and the strong, syrupy, chicory-laced coffee favored in Chennai. What I wanted was both more and less. I wanted India to be the kind of different world that I could take part in. I wanted to feel myself moving differently through life, ever so slightly but still noticeably, and on that score too India did not disappoint me.

Our plane got in around four in the morning, and by ten I was ready to see some of Chennai. (The coffee took care of any jet lag.) My plan was to visit Higgenbotham's, the doyen of the city's many English-language bookstores, and after checking with the front desk about the appropriate autorickshaw fare I went out.

I had read in the always-trustworthy *Lonely Planet* guidebook that nothing can prepare the traveler for his or her first days in India. Counting on *Lonely Planet* as I did, I expected to be disoriented if not overwhelmed. I was not. What surprised me most was that everything I saw made sense. It was indeed a different kind of sense from the one I was used to, but it was easy to grasp and doing so was pleasurable and even exhilarating. It was also deeply illuminating.

There was the traffic, for example. To the degree that India is motorized it is a noisy place, and this makes Chennai a *very* noisy place indeed. Traffic on the main roads is a teeming, honking chaos. Trucks, local buses and air-conditioned luxury coaches, late model cars, elderly Ambassador taxis, motorcycles and bicycles, pert yellow exhaust-spewing autorickshaws and environmentally correct autorickshaws run on natural gas, death-defying pedestrians, and even the occasional bullock cart that seems to have strayed in from a tourist snapshot, all weave and jostle for position amid a continuous din of sounding horns. Most of the racket is made up of straightforward factory-issue honks, but a few creative drivers, not content with personalizing their vehicles with ornate lettering and painted flowers and gods, play tunes or military-style salutes.

Horns find uses in India to which they are not put in the West. Where I come from hearing a horn is a sign that something is wrong. In India you sound your horn routinely. As I realized even during my first morning's ride to the bookstore, it's a signal that you're about to overtake or pass someone else. Many of the trucks I saw requested this; amid the decorative flowers and greenery on the back gates the drivers had painted "Sound horn."

I could have shrugged this off as a minor cultural difference with no deep meaning attached to it. But I am the kind of person who's always looking for the deep meanings behind everything that people do, and I began to notice that honking-as-signaling fit in with other quirks. Hardly anyone paid attention to the lane markings, for one thing, and disregard of traffic signals was so common that I saw signs that earnestly requested of motorists that they stop at red lights. It clearly did little good. Our excellent and safety-conscious bus drivers simply drove through intersections when nobody was visible on the cross streets.

But what I was seeing was not really chaos. It had its own coherence. The drivers were actually being very attentive; they were always watching each other and adjusting to the moment-by-moment flow of the traffic. Every move was a counter-move, depending on the situation as a whole as much as it did on where the drivers wanted to go. That's why the constant honking was necessary. It's how drivers became aware of those behind them.

The drivers, then, were creating their own kind of order. We think of order as something settled and linear, and as long as that's the only kind of order that you recognize you wouldn't see Chennai traffic as anything but a mess. On its own terms, however, it was totally organized. The difference is that the organization came from within. It was the constantly changing harmony of everyone's intentions playing off against everyone else's.

I saw this most clearly early in our trip, as our bus waited to make a right turn onto the road for Thiruvannamalai. As traffic in India moves on the left hand side, a right turn is a turn into traffic. Heading in from the side road was a mix of cars, trucks, buses, and motorcycles, and they were moving on both left and right sides of the road at once. For a moment or two we were witnessing a mashup of two incompatible traffic patterns.

It should have been terrifying, but I at least found it a joy to watch. Traffic was not as heavy here and I could watch each vehicle subtly shift, slow down, speed up, or swerve in response to the others. As in some intricate dance, choreographed by someone with a taste for the outrageous but not for the random, the patterns traced by the drivers were both unpredictable and deliberate.

I'm an inveterate generalizer and I couldn't help but see this as a real insight into Indian life. The way people related to rules was different here, I thought. Traditional Indian life had lots of rules, of course—many more than European cultures did—but all of them were personalized. That's because everyone was supposed to live the life that was defined by his or her specific social role. This was your *dharma,* and no one-size-fits-all *dharma* exists. Instead, there are different *dharmas* for every caste and every group. Merchants have one *dharma* and priests have another. *Dharma* is different for tailors and cobblers, for leather-workers and for dung collectors. Men and women follow different rules, and there are rules that apply to first-born sons and rules that govern their younger brothers. And every rule has its exceptions and everything is always subject to negotiation—even caste, which scholars tell us was much more fluid until the British came along. Everything returns, ultimately, to the give-and-take of everyday life.

Rules made this way weren't and aren't abstract. The English rulers of India complained that the idea of general laws that applied impartially to everyone seemed alien to their Indian subjects. But they were unable to see that Indian life hung together differently. It was built on concrete exchanges among real people. The result, at its best, was and is a self-generating, living, constantly changing kind of organization.

As nice as it sounds, this kind of organization has its problems. As everyone who's tried to use it in political contexts knows, it's all too easily subverted by anyone who's more interested in power than in process. There are times when Indian traffic is terrifying and the interplay turns deadly. In any case, India is no more consistent than any other place. Along with self-generated order you'll find hierarchy, class and sexual oppression, institutionalized inequality, and communal violence. Corruption and cronyism are far too common and lineage and caste are still important. Indian life can sometimes turn a real free-for-all, where respect, recognition, and power appear to justify themselves. Many are left behind, powerless and voiceless.

But the order I saw in the traffic comes from something real and distinctive, too, and it's one of the aspects of Indian culture that attracted me most. I was not alone. One of the ladies on our trip told me, "I've lived in India and America. Both are good, but in India I feel....I feel *freer*." She could have been talking about the lack of government regulation, I suppose; another woman told me that her children loved to come to India because they didn't have to wear seat belts in the car. But I don't think that's what she meant. I think she felt more at home in the world when she was there, less separated from everyone around her, more present in the give-and-take of life. Her world

In the land of temples, page 57

was more open, less hemmed in—not because she had her way in everything but because she could play a role in deciding how things were for everyone.

I felt that, too. When order comes from below it doesn't impose itself on us. It becomes something that we make, something intimately our own. In India everything is personal—even the price you pay in a shop, which reflects the play of intention and skill between shopkeeper and buyer. Your voice may be big or small, you may pay too much or get a real bargain, but regardless of the outcome you're still part of the conversation.

The Western world is different. The flip side of the inner self we cherish in our hearts is the blank impersonality of the world that confronts us with its expectations, rules, and demands. That world cares little or nothing for our own needs and wishes. It seems to come from nowhere; it's simply *there*. You can't talk with it, and changing it is the hardest of uphill fights. The best we can do is come to terms with it, or limit its power.

Think in terms of self and other, mind and world, inner truth and outward show; however you imagine it, life in the West is worked out between individuals on the one side, struggling to be true to their inner natures, and something unyielding—society, the law, reality—on the other. Whatever our political or social stance, we end up thinking of the world as something that exists apart from us, so much so that joining it seems almost optional. If the world is sensibly organized we get benefits from it, so we're encouraged to give back to it, and if it's badly organized we can try to change it. But our true home is the self. Our deepest need is for the room in which it can flourish, a space free from worldly pressures, and we struggle to defend that space. The world pushes against us and we push back. Neither side will budge, and the battle is exhausting.

This separation simply isn't as strong in India. Self and world mix into each other, sometimes so thoroughly that you can't tell them apart. You're not expected to carve out room for your individual life. This sounds terrifying to some people, and at its worst it can indeed crush the spirit; one has only to look at the lives of poor Indian peasants and slum-dwellers, especially women and especially in the impoverished parts of the country. But it can also be liberating, because what vanishes in that mix is not the self or the world, what vanishes is the delusion that these exist apart from each other. We can stop wasting our time and energy maintaining an imaginary separation. We don't need to defend our self, because there's nothing there to defend. We can let it change with every interaction and take pleasure in the ways in which the world changes along with it. Self-transformation isn't any kind of exceptional accomplishment, then. It can be the very essence of daily life.

This insight is at the heart of most Indian religious traditions, including the Sufism that was long the most popular form of Islam in the subcontinent. Self and world, individual and society, humanity and the gods—all separations are unreal. Every difference is temporary and unimportant. Everything that we see and everything that we are, have been, and will be is all part of a single process. In Hindu terms it's *lila*, the playful self-expression of the divine. You and I are part of that play. Indeed, there is nothing else.

I suspect that this is why India can seem overwhelmingly frenetic and quietly calm at the same time. It is the teeming, noisy, constantly-changing manifestation of something that people understand as timeless and silent. Everything bumps up against everything else, but the other isn't so strongly other and the self isn't so strongly the self. There's less at stake. Life is more intimate and more casual. The ideal is to let go entirely, and though few people attain that ideal it's still easier to let go when that's what you know you should do. You win and you lose, people arrive and depart, you're born and you die. There are no final scores. There is no finality; death is never the end. What counts is how fully engaged you are in the process.

An eminent Indian psychiatrist and author, Sudhir Kakar, argued years ago that this was one of India's biggest problems. People didn't function so well outside of their communities, he said, because they didn't see themselves as individuals and couldn't make independent decisions the way Westerners did. (The past twenty years of development may have changed his thinking about that.) But whatever its impact on the economy, the way self and world flow into each other in India is more than a religious idea or a cultural quirk. Many scientists in the West have come to think that the independent, individual self that we cling to and defend is an illusion, which is exactly what Indians of every religious tradition have always told us.

The Western approach, binding separate lives together with abstract rules, may be better at limiting abuses of power. But it has its own dangers—which is just what you would expect if that separation is a delusion. It makes our involvement in social life seem like a choice instead of a fact, with dreadful effects on our politics. It hides oppression behind the veil of a neutral, impersonal set of rules; as Anatole France once said, "The law, in its majestic equality, forbids the rich and the poor alike to sleep under bridges, to beg in the streets, and to steal bread." And by basing social life on the assumption that everyone is ultimately self-interested, don't we run the risk of turning ourselves into our own nightmare? If our only social principles are dedicated to keeping people apart from each other, do we actually encourage self-interest, alienation, loneliness, and evil?

I won't try to answer any of these questions. I know only that there is something deeply seductive about the everyday life that I saw and felt in the streets of Chennai. Another Indian friend, raised in a suburb of Rochester and to the ear as typical an American twenty-something as you could hope to meet, said to me, "Every time I get back to the States I think, 'Why am I doing this? Why didn't I just stay?'" She did not tell me more, but I think I understand. The ever-changing order which is the very music of life, the divine play that constantly gives birth to everything and sweeps everything back into itself—the gods' *lila*—seems closer to the surface there, sometimes so close it is almost tangible. There is one virtue in Indian life that outweighs its obvious problems: the refusal to make those separations that we rely on in the West. That's why the structure and grounding of Indian life, its pleasures, and its miseries, are indeed more firmly rooted in reality. We are not separate from each other or from the world, after all, and we are not separate from the gods, either. Our world is no different from theirs. Guruji, Aiya's guru, put it perfectly to us at

In the land of temples, page 60

the beginning of our pilgrimage. "You have all this freedom," he said, "you can do anything and become anything. And why does god give you this freedom? He has no choice. He is you."

Silk store, Chennai, Tamil Nadu

Panagal Park, Chennai, in a cyclone

Outside Nemili, Tamil Nadu

Rice paddies, coconut palms

The dance of Shiva

Aiya, Chidambaram, Tamil Nadu

In the land of temples, page 73

Chidambaram should have been the high point of our pilgrimage. Famous throughout India, it is the spiritual heart of the Tamil world; when South Indians say "the Temple" it's Chidambaram that they're talking about. Once a flimsy shelter in a forest of thorn trees, it was built up into the most splendid of temples by the kings of the fabled Chola dynasty a thousand years ago. It is there that they were crowned, and it is there that some of the greatest devotional poetry in Tamil literature was composed. And it was there that Shiva danced.

If you're familiar with any piece of South Indian art it's probably the image of Shiva Nataraja, Shiva as the lord of the dance. As a ring of fire expands behind his slim body he crushes the dwarfish figure of ignorance with one foot and offers the other as refuge. In two of his four hands he holds a drum and a flame, creating and dissolving the world in the same moment, and the other two hands point to his upraised foot and gesture to us to have no fear.

The stories of the gods are gloriously, exuberantly inconsistent, and there are any number of accounts of the "real" dance of Shiva. Some people will tell you that the image depicts a dance in a cremation ground, far away from Chidambaram. But you don't need to decide which story to believe. The world is nothing but Shiva and all of its movement and change is his dance. All of the stories are true, at least if they help you to see that deeper truth.

As Aiya tells it, Lord Shiva came to the inhospitable wilderness where the temple now stands when the goddess Kali, the resident deity in the area, saw him dancing and challenged him to a contest. He accepted her challenge and proposed that each one would duplicate or better the other's moves. Kali agreed to this condition, and as he danced the god kicked one leg up over his head. To do the same would have been too great a breach of female modesty even for Kali. Rather than commit such an indecency she conceded defeat and retreated to the outskirts of the town, content to serve Shiva as a guardian deity.

Since that day Shiva has been venerated in Chidambaram as Shiva Nataraja. Instead of the *lingam* at the heart of the sanctuary there is a *murti* of the dancing god. This alone sets the temple in Chidambaram apart from every other Shiva temple in India.

There is a *lingam* in Chidambaram, though—but it is unique as well. Like the big temple in Thiruvannamalai and several of the other temples that we visited, Chidambaram houses one of the elemental *lingams*, the *butalingas*. This one, though, is the most rarefied of all. It is the *lingam* of space, or ether, and to the eye and touch it is not there at all. It is found (if you can call it that) in the *rahasya*. The word means "secret," and it designates an area next to Shiva Nataraja which is curtained with hanging golden bilva leaves, the leaves of the plant most sacred to the god. After the priests show the *arati* fire to the dancer they bring it behind the golden leaves and shine it on the invisible *lingam* of space. Then they bring it out to the devotees.

The priests, too, are a group found only in Chidambaram. They are *dikshitars*, a hereditary group, nominally three thousand strong, that claims descent from Shiva's own retinue. (No self-respecting Indian god or king would be without his entourage.) Indeed, a famous story relates that one of the Chola kings prepared three thousand munificent gifts for the *dikshitars* and distributed them only to find that he had one left over. The identity of the missing priest was soon revealed; it was Lord Shiva himself who announced that he, too, was in their number. An egalitarian, self-governing community, the *dikshitars* were managing the temple and conducting its rituals as far back as records and memories reach.

I was eager to see the temple, to stand close to the statue of Shiva and to see the light dance in the *rahasya*. I am sure everyone else on our trip felt the same, and there was almost palpable disappointment the day before our visit when Aiya announced that we were not to have special *darshan*, were not to speak with any of the *dikshitars*, and were not to expect much of anything from our short stay. His spiritual advisor, herself an avatar of the Goddess, had told him that this was how it should be.

The reasons for this were not religious but political. The *dikshitars* are said to have come down to earth along with Lord Shiva, but the more prosaic explanation for their presence in Chidambaram is that they were Brahmins from North India, brought to this site by Tamil monarchs who wanted the prestige that patronizing Sanskrit and Vedic religion would provide. By the last century, though, popular Tamil politics had turned nationalist and often anti-Brahmin. Besides, the temple at Chidambaram is thought to be exceedingly wealthy. It became an obvious target for populist governments.

Most temples in India are under the control of the state, but the *dikshitars* had managed to maintain their independence by arguing that they themselves were a special religious denomination. This argument had won them a court battle in the 1980s, but a few years ago the issue heated up again. Conflicts broke out over a non-*dikshitar's* singing of Tamil hymns in the inner sanctuary during the *puja* itself. Not even other *dikshitars* are allowed to interrupt the *puja*, and they opposed what they saw as an invasion of their prerogatives. The Tamil Nadu government, though, took the side of the hymn singer, who of course was not Brahmin, and the police were brought in. Then, in 2009, the government simply took over the temple, leaving the *dikshitars* to carry out the rituals under state supervision. The case is still in court.

There was not really much for the state to take over. Less than four hundred *dikshitars* remain, and most of them are poor. There are complaints of their importuning visitors and soliciting money, but the average *dikshitar's* family lives on less than fifty dollars a month. Donations are their only source of support. Being so few and so impoverished, they have struggled to keep the buildings in repair while resisting the ticket system for special darshan and other privileges that keeps other Hindu temples solvent. Government officials have said that they simply wanted the temple run more efficiently.

Whatever the government's motives, Aiya wanted to do nothing that would seem to ratify the takeover. We would visit, but we would hold ourselves apart. There was nothing we could do. It was clear that this would not be the experience that we or he had hoped for, and in the early morning light we trooped uneasily through the streets towards the great temple *gopuram*.

There was much that was awe-inspiring. The towers and sanctuaries had a grandeur befitting royal patronage; only Ekambareshwara in the ancient Chola capital of Kanchipuram was comparable. As we entered we heard peals of bells, incongruously cathedral-like. By the time we reached the sanctuary the noise was overwhelming. I looked behind as we walked in and saw one large bell and a rack of smaller ones in an alcove, swinging away as unseen bell-ringers pulled the ropes. It was like worshiping in a bell tower.

The sanctuary was once a thatched hut, and even today it has the shape and the scale of a little shelter thrown up by devotees to protect their beloved *murti* from the rain. It is a stone hut these days, and for a millennium its roof has been hammered gold instead of thatch. Yet there is still something touchingly modest about the sanctuary at Chidambaram, and it feels more open to the world than the womb-like structures at the other great temples.

Even this early the crowds were thick. We stood below, as Aiya had told us, rather than up at the level of the sanctuary itself. I had only poor view of the *murti* of the dancing god. As the priest began his ritual a man next to me tried to explain things. I thought he was telling me when the priest was in the *rahasya*, but between his Tamil-accented English and the chiming of the bells it was hard for me to know what he meant. I am still not sure that I saw it. I am still not sure what was going on.

Then we were outside, following Aiya as he tried to bring us to other parts of the complex. But he found his way blocked by gates and fences that had not been there on his earlier visits. Nothing was as it had been. The rituals continued, but it was obvious that for Aiya, at least, the spirit was missing. I do not know how much was my own perception and how much was picked up from Aiya's sadness, but the great courtyards of the temple felt forlorn. Laundry hung in one of the halls, grass grew amid the paving stones, and it was a government functionary, not a priest, who unlocked the Ganesh temple near the entrance.

In the land of temples, page 78

We walked back more quietly than we had come. Our spirits revived at the Kali temple, the little shrine where she was said to have withdrawn after Shiva's questionable victory. Off in a sanctuary to the side, wearing a white sari and drenched in red *kumkum* except for her pleading, piercing eyes, Kali at least seemed unconcerned with government edict. And that was it. The buses took us to our hotel in Pondicherry, then back to Chennai, where an impromptu visit to the beach helped us let go of the tension and disappointment that remained. Off on his own Aiya performed a quiet ritual, offering up what merit had been accumulated in our pilgrimage for the benefit of the world. It is not good to do any of this for yourself alone, and it is not good to try to hold on to experiences, even the good and illuminating ones.

In the land of temples, page 79

That ended our pilgrimage, at least formally. Mine, though, had one more destination. The next day was our last in India—our departing flight left at an ungodly hour and the buses were set to bring us to the airport at eleven o'clock that night. The day was set aside for packing and last-minute shopping, and in the morning a single bus took a few of us to the Mylapore district, to the streets around the Kapaleeshwara Temple. It was a sensible destination, because the temple was in the middle of a lively commercial district where we could shop for jewelry, books, CDs, dance costumes and music, religious articles, and silks. It was also next to a branch of Hotel Saranava Bhavan, a first-rate chain of "high class vegetarian restaurants." I wanted one more South Indian meal.

Kapaleeshwara fills a city block but it's simple as large temples go. There is a wall, almost concealed behind the proliferation of shops and stalls, and a decently large *gopuram*, but most of the the sanctuaries were gathered back to back in the middle of a single courtyard. There were none of the elaborate nesting enclosures of the big temple in Tiruvannamalai or the royal establishments in Kanchipuram or Chidambaram. It felt more like a larger version of the innumerable street corner temples found throughout Chennai.

I was alone, dressed in Indian clothes, and was free to wander and linger. It was a perfect day, too—warm and breezy, the sun strong in a clear blue sky. I had darshan of Shiva and Devi, leaving a ten-rupee note for each priest as I took in the light and accepted pinches of *vibhuti* ash and *kumkum*. Nobody paid me any special attention. I was just another one of the devotees who streamed in and out to spend a few moments in the presence of the gods. I could imagine myself that way, at least, and nobody there was unfriendly or ill-willed enough to treat me otherwise.

In the land of temples, page 80

    I try to do *japam* every day, which generally means 108 repetitions of the most important of the mantras that I've been given. The temple seemed like the right place to do that, so I found a spot with a pillar to support my back as I faced the weathered black stone Shiva temple. I pull out my counting beads, my *mala*, and start. It's neither more nor less absorbing than when I do it at home but it still feels right to be sitting here.

    About halfway through a circle of women, mostly in their forties or older, gather behind me, sit down, and pull out booklets. The settle down to sing devotional songs in Tamil. My concentration wavers, but then my concentration is always wavering, and I make it through the last repetition of my mantra and allow myself to listen to their sweet, earnest voices. Then I get up again and wander around the courtyard.

In the land of temples, page 81

On one side of the main sanctuaries I look into an overgrown garden with a small stone Nandi in the middle. Behind me families are lined up for *iddly* from the temple kitchen, the spongy white cakes, made from fermented rice and lentil flour, that with a spicy vegetable sauce called *sambar* is the favorite breakfast in South India. People stream in and out of the main temples with bags of flowers and *bilva* leaves and walk prayerfully around the brightly-painted smaller shines. Devotees light little clay lamps filled with ghee and offer prayers to the images carved into the temple's columns. Families watch their children at play in the shade of the pillared halls. I realize that the temple is also something of a public park, something spiritual and urban at once, a place for both recreation and re-creation.

On the other side of the sanctuaries there is a small bower with a few cows. One priest offers a libation at the base of a sacred tree. Another leads a class through Sanskrit chants in a study hall built up against the outer wall. I don't have anything that I need to do there but it's so pleasant to take in the activity around me that I can't leave. A young men chats with me for a few minutes and hands me a small bowl of *prasadam*, food from the temple that has first been offered to the gods. I thank him and devour it. I can't tell what it is but it's delicious.

I really did have some last-minute shopping to do, though, and I finally admit that it was time for me to go. At the same time I realized that this too is what I was supposed to do. There is no separation, after all. You walk into the temple to stand at the point where everything is unified beyond any idea we could ever have of unity, and then you walk out again through the *gopuram* into the world that unfolds from that point and is not apart from it. The temple needs its city just as the city needs its temples. It is only when they're together that we live in what the Greeks and Romans called "the common city of gods and men."

The Greeks and Romans, even the Babylonians, would have felt at home here. Their temple worship was an altogether bloodier affair, but their temples themselves were not so different and they would have little trouble figuring out the point of the rituals. Their temples, too—like the temple in Jerusalem—were good places to eat, and they too were surrounded by the stalls of shopkeepers selling offerings, trinkets, snacks, and souvenirs. Their gods, too, went out in chariots at festival time to survey their domains.

This, I felt, was how it has always been done. We all live in the presence of the gods. There is nothing but their play, the dance of Shiva; if you want to be rationalistic about it, there is nothing but the intricate and infinite process that becomes you and me and everything else. But we draw away from that knowledge, especially as we indulge in what we like to call progress, so for millennia we have built temples to transform the way we see and live so we can sense it once again. The temple walls concentrate that taste of reality. Its gates let us in so we can feel it on the tips of our tongues and let us out again so we can carry it within ourselves. Many people have forgotten how important that is, but it is not forgotten here. I look forward to returning.

About the author

Michael Steinberg is an independent scholar and writer living in Rochester, New York, where he works as a lawyer. He is the author of *The Fiction of a Thinkable World: Body, Meaning, and the Culture of Capitalism* (Monthly Review Press, 2005) and *A New Biology of Religion: Spiritual Practice and the Life of the Body* (Praeger, forthcoming). He has taught at the University of Rochester and published essays on the philosophy of German Idealism. He is also an initiate at the Sri Rajarajeswari Peetham in Rush, New York, and blogs occasionally on religion, science, and social issues at http://open.salon.com/blog/mlstein. He and his wife, the photographer Loret Steinberg, are under the close supervision of two medium-haired cats.